Understanding Sexual Identity and Orientation

Kris Hirschmann

San Diego, CA

© 2018 ReferencePoint Press, Inc.
Printed in the United States

For more information, contact:
ReferencePoint Press, Inc.
PO Box 27779
San Diego, CA 92198
www.ReferencePointPress.com

LIBRARY OF CONGRESS CATALOGING-IN-PUBLICATION DATA

Name: Hirschmann, Kris, 1967– author.
Title: Understanding Sexual Identity and Orientation/by Kris Hirschmann.
Description: San Diego, CA: ReferencePoint Press, Inc., [2018] | Series:
    Understanding psychology | Includes bibliographical references and index.
    Identifiers: LCCN 2017014674 (print) | LCCN 2017020915 (ebook) | ISBN
    9781682822821 (eBook) | ISBN 9781682822814 (hardback)
Subjects: LCSH: Sexual orientation—Juvenile literature. | Gender
    identity—Juvenile literature. | Sexual minorities—Identity—Juvenile
    literature.
Classification: LCC HQ18.5 (ebook) | LCC HQ18.5 .H57 2018 (print) | DDC
    306.76--dc23
LC record available at https://lccn.loc.gov/2017014674

CONTENTS

The Human Brain: Thought, Behavior, and Emotion

Frontal lobe controls:
- Thinking
- Planning
- Organizing
- Problem solving
- Short-term memory
- Movement
- Personality
- Emotions
- Behavior
- Language

Parietal lobe:
- Interprets sensory information, such as taste, temperature, and touch

Temporal lobe:
- Processes information from the senses of smell, taste, and sound
- Plays role in memory storage

Occipital lobe:
- Processes images from the eyes
- Links information with images stored in memory

Source: Mayo Foundation for Education and Research, "Slide Show: How Your Brain Works." www.mayoclinic.org.

INTRODUCTION

What Are Sexual Identity and Orientation?

A man named Daniel clearly remembers the moment he realized he was attracted to women. A little girl in his first grade class spoke to him, and in that instant his whole world changed. "It was as if a droplet of boiling hot oil had been dropped into the pool of water in my deepest self, spattered and swam, and made me dizzy. I felt confusing desires and weird attractions. I felt drawn. In that moment, I knew: I liked girls and I wanted their attention,"[1] he says. Daniel subsequently followed a typical path of development and matured into a heterosexual (attracted to the opposite sex) adult.

The situation was totally different for another man who has chosen to remain anonymous. "I knew I was different from a very early age. Children can always tell when they're not like other kids," he recalls. "I preferred playing with girls and was more interesting in girly things than boy things, and I knew that wasn't normal. I had crushes on other boys and was fascinated by men's bodies."[2] This man continued to have feelings of same-sex attraction as he grew, and he eventually matured into a homosexual (attracted to the same sex) adult.

These two men grew up in the same society and were reared according to similar values. Yet the ways they think and feel about themselves in terms of their sexuality are very different. These types of thoughts and feelings fall under the blanket terms of *sexual orientation* and *sexual identity*—psychological concepts that describe people's sexual feelings, beliefs, and self-concepts.

Sexual Orientation vs. Identity

Before diving into any examination of sexual orientation and identity, it is important to understand the difference between these terms. *Sexual orientation* and *sexual identity* are often discussed together, and although they are closely related, they are not the same.

> **WORDS IN CONTEXT**
>
> **sexual orientation**
> A person's enduring patterns of emotional, romantic, and/or sexual attraction.
>
> **sexual identity**
> The way a person thinks about and expresses the sexual aspects of his or her personality.

Sexual orientation, according to the American Psychological Association, is defined as "an enduring pattern of emotional, romantic, and/or sexual attractions to men, women, or both sexes."[3] It is distinct from other components of sex and gender, including a person's biological sex, gender identity (the psychological sense of being male or female), and social gender role (the cultural norms that define feminine and masculine behavior). In the simplest terms, sexual orientation is what turns a person on.

The term *sexual identity* refers to the way people think and feel about themselves as sexual beings. It typically aligns closely with sexual orientation, particularly in people who identify as heterosexual—in other words, people who feel only opposite-sex attraction virtually always think of themselves as heterosexual. The picture is a bit muddier for nonheterosexual people. People who feel same-sex attraction might see themselves as homosexual, bisexual (feeling attracted to both sexes), or essentially straight but perhaps a little curious.

A key difference between sexual orientation and identity is the element of personal choice. Science suggests that people cannot control or change their sexual feelings. They can, however, control how they think about these feelings and how they behave in response to them. Determining which parts are fixed and which are changeable is a major, ongoing topic of study in the field of sexual orientation and identity.

Gender Identity

Gender identity is yet another piece of the puzzle and is not the same as either sexual identity or sexual orientation. This term refers to how people feel about their gender and whether they identify themselves as male or female.

The vast majority of people feel aligned with their birth gender. In psychological terms, they are said to be cisgender. This means they were born with a certain body, and they are comfortable in it. So in

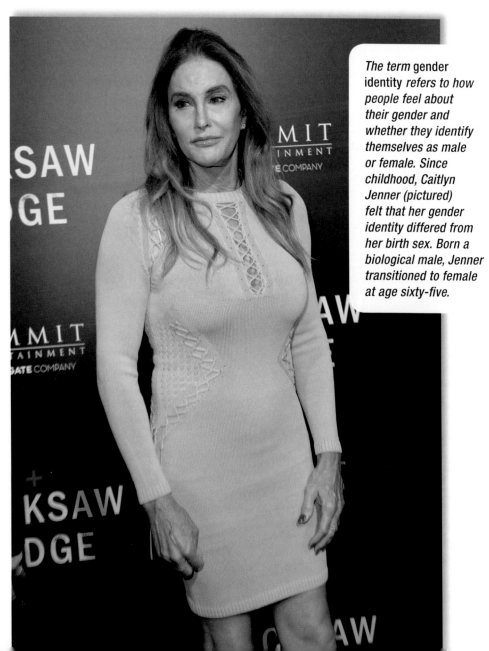

The term gender identity *refers to how people feel about their gender and whether they identify themselves as male or female. Since childhood, Caitlyn Jenner (pictured) felt that her gender identity differed from her birth sex. Born a biological male, Jenner transitioned to female at age sixty-five.*

other words, most biological males think of themselves as males; most biological females think of themselves as females. These feelings are not related to a person's sexual orientation or identity. A biological male who thinks of himself as male may be heterosexual or nonheterosexual. Likewise, a biological female who thinks of herself as female may also be heterosexual or nonheterosexual.

A small percentage of people—about 0.6 percent of the US population, according to a 2016 national survey of state demographic data—do not fit the cisgender mold. They feel that their physical gender does not match their mental and/or emotional gender. In other words, their gender identity differs from their biological sex. Strictly speaking, this aspect of a person's identity is not related to sexuality. Because it falls outside the heterosexual norm, however, it is usually included in discussions of sexual orientation and identity.

Freedom to Question

Historically, society's willingness to accept varying sexual orientations and identities has differed dramatically from one time and place to another. The social atmosphere has ranged from very open to very restrictive and sometimes even punitive toward those who fall outside the norm. In modern Western nations, the trend has been toward an increasingly liberal viewpoint. As sexual differences have become more and more accepted, it has become less intimidating for individuals of all orientations and identities to question their sexuality—and to be open with themselves and others about the answers they find.

Increased openness does not mean that the road to self-knowledge is easy. It can be confusing, difficult, and isolating to be a member of any minority group—a label that definitely applies to nonheterosexual people. But overwhelmingly, people who have come to terms with their nonheterosexual status say that the rewards far outweigh the costs. As difficult as it can be, the journey is usually rewarding for anyone who seeks to truly understand and accept his or her sexual orientation and identity.

CHAPTER 1

Defining Sexual Identity

At one time, not long ago, defining sexual identity was a fairly straightforward matter. People were considered to be either straight (heterosexual) or gay (homosexual), and the question mostly ended there.

The situation is different today. Subgroups within the non-heterosexual community now use many different terms to define themselves. The commonly used abbreviation LGBTQ+ covers the major groups. The five initial letters stand for *lesbian, gay, bisexual, transgender*, and *queer*, and the plus sign stands for everything else. An examination of these categories is helpful in understanding how people define their sexual identities.

The Heterosexual Majority

Heterosexuals make up by far the largest category of sexual identity. So-called classic heterosexuals, in psychological terms, are cisgender people who feel sexually attracted only to the opposite sex and who think of themselves in those terms. In other words, they are men who like women and women who like men. They report no feelings of same-sex attraction, and they are completely comfortable with their straight sexual identity.

The heterosexual category also includes people who feel some same-sex attraction but choose to identify themselves as straight anyway. The word *choose* in this context is important because sexual identity is largely under a person's control. People who feel same-sex attraction might identify as straight for countless reasons, including the relative strength of their attractions or societal and family pressures. One woman who falls into this category describes her feelings in an online forum. "I've always identified as heterosexual and have had a handful of boyfriends

and male sexual partners, but I became increasingly aware as I grew older that I was also attracted to women," she explains. But these feelings do not make her gay, she says, "because there's a difference between finding someone attractive and wanting to act on it."[4]

Putting aside the precise makeup of someone's so-called straightness, there is much debate concerning the percentage of self-identified heterosexual people, and many scientific studies have tried to pin down the answer to this question. Results have varied depending on countless factors, including when and where the studies were conducted. There is now enough data, however, for psychologists to feel fairly confident that the percentage of heterosexual humans hovers somewhere between 90 and 95 percent. In a world of about 7.5 billion people, that means somewhere between 6.75 billion and 7.1 billion people are straight. This means, of course, that up to 750 million people are not straight. Within this group, other definitions of sexual identity come into play.

L Is for Lesbian

The *L* in *LGBTQ+* stands for *lesbian*. Lesbians are women who feel emotionally and sexually attracted to other women. This term is derived from the name of the Greek island of Lesbos, which was home to a female poet named Sappho in the seventh and sixth centuries BCE. Sappho lived with a group of young women and wrote extensively about how much she loved them and admired

The Kinsey Scale

The Kinsey scale, also called the Heterosexual-Homosexual Rating Scale, was introduced in 1948 by an American scientist and sex researcher named Alfred Kinsey. Kinsey was one of the first scientists to propose that human sexuality existed on a continuum. He claimed that some people are exclusively heterosexual or homosexual, but many others fall somewhere in between.

Kinsey's scale rates sexual orientation on a scale of 0 to 6, as follows:

0   Exclusively heterosexual

1   Predominantly heterosexual, only incidentally homosexual

2   Predominantly heterosexual but more than incidentally homosexual

3   Equally heterosexual and homosexual

4   Predominantly homosexual but more than incidentally heterosexual

5   Predominantly homosexual, only incidentally heterosexual

6   Exclusively homosexual

The scale also accommodates people who report no interest in sex and no sexual interactions. This state, which is called asexuality, receives a Kinsey rating of X.

The Kinsey scale was controversial when it was introduced, but scientific thinking has changed since the 1940s, and the idea of sexuality as a continuum is well accepted today. By asking people to rate themselves according to Kinsey's categories, scientists can understand sexuality in a more nuanced way than they could if they simply asked whether people considered themselves gay or straight.

their bodies. Inspired by this literature, the word *lesbian* was first used in the late 1800s to describe same-sex female attraction and was eventually adopted by homosexual women as their preferred label.

There is no typical lesbian, and women who identify with this label may look, dress, and act in any way they choose. That said, however, the lesbian community does tend to divide itself into some self-described categories.

One such category goes by the nickname "butch." A butch lesbian is a woman who presents herself in a masculine way in

Lesbians who present themselves in a masculine way through dress, grooming, mannerisms, and other personal characteristics are categorized as butch. This manly behavior, however, does not reflect a desire to be a man.

her dress, grooming, speech, mannerisms, and other personal characteristics. This manly behavior does not reflect a desire to be a man; the butch lesbian identifies fully as a woman and is comfortable in her body. One butch woman explains her take on the matter: "[People] seem to think that I must 'want' to be a guy, because I look and act in more masculine ways. The truth is that I love being Butch. I am not afraid of my female parts. . . . I am fine with my masculine appearance and my butch ways."[5]

At the opposite end of the spectrum from the butch women are the femme lesbians, who sometimes also call themselves lipstick lesbians. Women who fall into this group choose to dress, act, and generally present themselves in a typically feminine way, but they still feel sexual and emotional attraction to other women. "I wear dresses, I love shopping and wearing makeup. That doesn't mean I'm any less of a lesbian," says one woman who expresses herself in feminine ways. "Being a lesbian . . . has nothing to do with how we dress, or do our hair. It is about the feelings we get when we are near a girl we like."[6]

Highly femme and highly butch lesbians might be said to fall at opposite extremes, with countless modes of self-expression in between—and many, many lesbians find their comfort zone somewhere in this middle ground. It is fair to say that identifying as a lesbian has little relation to a woman's personal style.

G Is for Gay

The G in LGBTQ+ stands for gay. This word can describe any member of the LGBTQ+ community, but it is most often used in reference to homosexual men. A gay man is someone who is biologically male and who identifies as such, but he is romantically and sexually attracted to other men.

This usage of the word gay is fairly recent, dating back to the mid-1950s. Before that time, the word meant mostly "happy" and "carefree," but it could also mean "licentious" (lacking moral restraints, particularly in sexual matters). Because homosexual men were once thought to embody this definition, the word *gay* began to take on its modern meaning. The word was originally meant as a slur, but today homosexual men everywhere proudly accept the label.

Like the lesbian community, the gay community has a number of subcategories that are widespread and well recognized. Within each category, self-appointed members choose to act and dress according to certain norms. Examples include bears, who are large, hairy, and masculine; twinks, who are young, slender, and clean-shaven; queens, who speak and behave in an exaggeratedly feminine way; leathermen, who wear provocative leather clothing to broadcast an interest in certain types of sexual activity; and muscle queens, who spend a great deal of time in the gym working to perfect their bodies.

By adopting the mannerisms and mores of these subcategories, some gay men find comfort and a sense of belonging and acceptance. But many others dislike the idea of being pigeonholed, and they resist all potentially stereotypical behavior. In a popular guidebook for LGBTQ+ teens, authors Kathy Belge and Marke Bieschke remind young gay men that it is okay to fit into a subculture—and it is also okay not to fit in. "Though you'll find evidence of a lot of these subcultures online and in most major cities, you don't have to belong to any of them," they write. "Remember, these identities are only to help gay men say a little about who they are to the world. Never take on an identity if you don't want to, or let others label you against your will."[7]

B Is for Bisexual

The *B* in *LGBTQ+* stands for *bisexual*. This term applies to both men and women. People who identify as bisexual, or bi, feel sexually and romantically drawn to partners of both sexes. They are comfortable acknowledging both types of attraction, and they have absorbed this aspect of themselves into their sexual self-image.

Sometimes people think that being bisexual means being equally attracted to both sexes. This can be true, but it is not always the case. Bisexual people frequently describe themselves

Dozens of Genders

Since its inception in 2004, Facebook has allowed users to identify themselves by gender. There were originally two choices: male or female. In 2014 the social media giant added a third custom category that offers more than fifty additional gender choices. Most are reasonably familiar or easy to figure out, including such choices as cisgender, transgender, transsexual, intersex, or neither. A few of the less intuitive, more exotic choices include the following:

agender: No specific gender identity.

androgyne: Having a specific combination of masculine and feminine characteristics.

gender fluid: A dynamic mix of male and female, changing in strength and balance from one moment or day to another.

neutrois: This may describe individuals who feel they fall outside traditional male/female boundaries.

pangender: Encompassing all genders.

two-spirit: A traditional role in some Native American tribes, descriptive of men with mixed gender identities.

By including these categories and others as gender choices, Facebook is acknowledging the many differences that exist among its nearly 2 billion subscribers—and making it possible for these people to broadcast this aspect of themselves along with their social communications.

as mostly heterosexual or mostly homosexual. This means they generally prefer men or women (depending on the gender of the speaker), but they have less intense or less frequent sexual feelings toward the other sex. They consider these feelings significant enough, however, to incorporate them into their sexual identity and define themselves accordingly.

It is also possible—and even frequent—for people to have both opposite-sex and same-sex attractions but *not* to identify as bisexual. These people often identify themselves as straight but somewhat interested in the idea or the experience of same-sex contact. This identification has become increasingly common in recent years, to the point that it now has a label: bicurious. Some people dismiss this concept and believe that so-called bicurious people are just fooling themselves, and they are actually bisexual. Other people accept the concept and argue that people have the right to choose their own labels, whatever their feelings may be. Either way, the phenomenon exists.

One common idea about bisexuality is that it is a stepping stone to being fully homosexual. In other words, people initially say they are bisexual and go through an experimental phase, then decide that they are really homosexual. Again, this is sometimes true, but not always. Many bisexuals remain firmly committed to a split sexual identity throughout their lives. "I'm a proud bisexual," proclaims one person who has no intention of swinging toward either end of the sexual identity spectrum. "I find both genders are so fascinating. Girls are so tender and sweet. Guys are so strong and wild. I enjoy the combination of both worlds. . . . They fit me the best."[8]

T Is for Transgender

The *T* in *LGBTQ+* stands for *transgender*, or *trans* for short. This term applies to people whose biological sex does not match their emotional or mental sex. Some transgender people are biological males who think and feel like females. These people are referred to as male-to-female, or MTF, transgender. Other transgender people are biological females who think and feel like males, and they are referred to as female-to-male, or FTM, transgender.

It is important to understand that being transgender is an entirely different issue from sexual orientation and identity. A transgender person of any biological sex may be sexually attracted to men, women, or both, and will develop a sexual identity based on his or her unique situation.

People who identify as transgender may choose to express their identity in countless ways. Some transgender people prefer not to call attention to themselves, so they act and dress in ways typical of their biological sex. Some may conform outwardly but feel most confident and alive when wearing undergarments that match their psychological gender. Some vary their style dramatically from one time to another, presenting themselves as male in some situations and female in others. And some commit fully to their transgender identity, presenting themselves as their preferred gender in all aspects of their lives.

People called transvestites are a subset of the transgender community. Transvestites are biological men who dress and present themselves as women. Some transvestites are performers who cross-dress as part of their act, and these people are known as drag queens.

Transsexuals are also a subset of the transgender community. A transsexual is someone who uses medical treatments, such as hormone therapy or surgery, to change the sexual characteristics of his or her body. A biological woman, for instance, might take a male hormone called testosterone to lower her voice, promote facial hair growth, and change certain body proportions. She might also opt for surgery to remove her breasts or to add male sexual organs. Likewise,

WORDS IN CONTEXT

transgender
Having a gender identity that does not match one's biological sex.

17

A teenager undergoing a female-to-male transition prepares an injection of the male hormone testosterone. Transsexuals may use hormone therapy to change the sexual characteristics of their bodies.

a biological male might take female hormones to promote feminine physical characteristics, or he might choose surgery to remove male organs or add female ones. These types of changes collectively are called transitioning. Not all trans people choose to transition, but those who do often say they feel better living in a body that matches their mental and emotional state of mind.

Q Is for Queer

The *Q* in *LGBTQ+* stands for *queer*. Many decades ago, this word meant anyone or anything that was a little bit unusual or out of the ordinary. In the late twentieth century, it came into use as a way to describe nonheterosexual people. It was originally meant as an insult, but as is the case with so many other derogatory terms, this one has been embraced by the LGBTQ+ community and is now a definition that many people choose for themselves.

The word *queer* is a slippery label in some ways because it is actually a nonlabel. It is used by people who feel that their sexuality or gender falls outside the heterosexual norm but who cannot or prefer not to pin it down further than that. "I feel that 'straight,' 'gay,' and 'bi' don't adequately cover or include the way I feel," explains one self-described queer person. "For me, identifying as queer is a way of placing myself outside straight, mainstream sexuality without having to identify with other ideas I can't relate to."[9]

Along with the word *queer*, the Q can also stand for *questioning*. This category of sexual identity is closely related to being queer because it indicates that someone is exploring his or her sexual feelings and is trying to sort out one's sexual identity. The difference between the two Qs is subtle, but it basically boils down to a person's progress along the path to self-knowledge. Queer people are choosing not to define themselves, but questioning people are not ready to do so.

WORDS IN CONTEXT

queer
An adjective that may describe anyone whose sexuality or gender falls outside the heterosexual norm.

Defining the Plus

The plus sign in *LGBTQ+* stands for everything else. It is a blanket symbol that can mean any type of outside-the-norm sexual identity not covered under the previous categories. So-called plus identities are much less common than any of the others, and they are often highly individualized. A few categories, however, are more common than others.

Pansexuality is one such category. A pansexual person is one who feels sexually attracted to people of any gender, gender identity, sexual orientation, or sexual identity. Perhaps the most famous pansexual person is singer and actress Miley Cyrus, who says she realized she was "pan" after meeting a gender-neutral person. "Looking at them, they were both [male and female]: beautiful and sexy and tough but vulnerable and feminine but masculine. And I related to that person more than I related to anyone in my life," she said in a 2016 interview. "I realized that's why I don't feel straight and I don't feel gay. Because I'm not."[10]

On the other end of the spectrum is asexuality, an identity adopted by some people who feel no interest in sex with partners of any gender or orientation. Asexual people are capable of romantic feelings and may enter intimate relationships. They may even have sex with their partners out of curiosity, to have children, or for a variety of other personal reasons. But their physical and emotional desire for sexual contact is completely absent.

People who define themselves as intersex form yet another group that falls under the plus. These people's bodies are biologically mixed, usually from birth, with some male and some female characteristics. Being intersex is a physical state and therefore is not a choice, but people with mixed biology do have a choice about how they define themselves, and for this reason the intersex label can be considered a type of sexual identity.

Choosing a Label

All of the terms discussed in this chapter have something in common: they are labels that people may choose to apply to themselves. Many people find these labels useful because they are shortcuts that help them to explain themselves to the rest of the world. When a person says "I'm straight," "I'm a lesbian," "I'm gay," or "I'm bisexual," other people have a general idea of what that means.

Just because labels exist, however, does not mean that anyone is obliged to adopt them. Each person has the right to form a unique sexual identity and an equal right to describe it however he or she wishes—or not to describe it at all. Labels, after all, are just words, and they are a shallow aspect of anyone's true sexual identity.

CHAPTER 2

What Determines Sexual Orientation?

Long before a person forms a sexual identity or adopts a label to describe it, he or she will experience sexual feelings. The type of sexual feelings a person has, and the people they are directed toward, is called a person's sexual orientation. Sexual orientation is not something a person decides; it just is what it is. This means that in any given person's mind, some types of people have natural appeal as sexual partners and others do not.

The question of what determines sexual orientation has been debated for thousands of years. Some people have argued that sexual orientation is fixed at or before birth, but others have said that it is learned. Countless scientific studies have tried to prove both viewpoints. None has provided a definitive answer, but many clues have been uncovered over the years. Although the precise formula remains elusive, not to mention hotly debated, scientists today largely agree that sexual orientation springs from a complicated mixture of biological and environmental factors.

Genetic Factors

The burning question for many scientists is whether sexual orientation has a genetic basis—in other words, whether it is actually written in people's genes as part of their biological structure. Although no one has been able to conclusively answer this question, there is considerable evidence that genetics do, in fact, play at least some part—and perhaps a large one—in sexual orientation.

DNA analysis is one line of study that has yielded interesting results. In 1993, a study of seventy-six gay brothers and their families revealed that the men had significantly more gay relatives on their mother's side of the family than on their father's side. Scientific equipment and procedures were then used to analyze these men's DNA (a molecule found in all cells that carries an organism's genetic code). The analysis showed that most of the men had a certain gene on a part of the DNA called the X chromosome, which is inherited from a man's mother. The study's authors felt this gene might be linked to sexual orientation. If this was the case, they said, it would be evidence that sexual orientation could be inherited from one's parents, particularly through the maternal line.

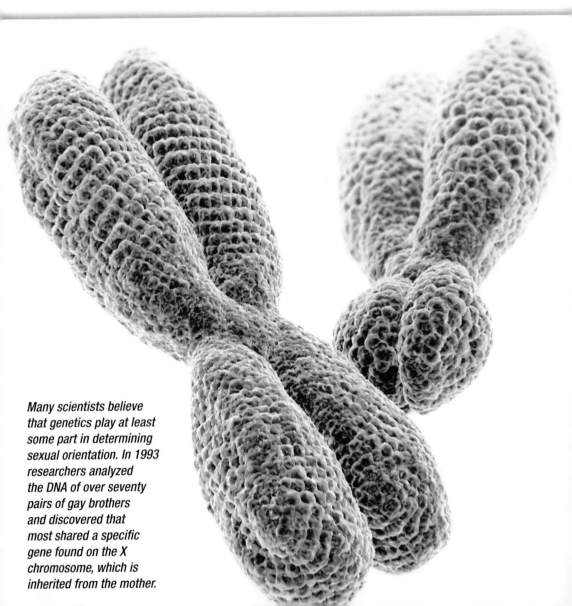

Many scientists believe that genetics play at least some part in determining sexual orientation. In 1993 researchers analyzed the DNA of over seventy pairs of gay brothers and discovered that most shared a specific gene found on the X chromosome, which is inherited from the mother.

Subsequent studies on this so-called gay gene had mixed results. Some scientists replicated the findings, but others did not. Still others found different genes in different places on the X chromosome that they claimed were linked to sexual orientation. The lack of clear answers led to a great deal of argument. In 2012, however, a major new piece of evidence was introduced into the debate by the largest study to date, which analyzed the DNA of 409 gay men. The analysis strongly supported the 1993 findings, discovering specific genetic patterns in the same place on the X chromosome. "Our findings, taken in context with previous work, suggest that genetic variation in each of these regions contributes to development of the important psychological trait of male sexual orientation,"[11] the study's authors concluded.

Studies of Twins

If sexual orientation is truly written in one's genes, it stands to reason that identical twins, who have identical DNA, should share this trait along with hair color, height, and other physical characteristics. A number of well-publicized studies, including a major 2010 survey of seventy-six hundred sets of fraternal and identical adult twins living in Sweden, have examined this question. They have found that identical twins do not, in fact, automatically have the same sexual orientation—but they do show a great deal of similarity in this area. Fifty-two percent of the identical twins of homosexual men were likewise homosexual. By contrast, only 22 percent of the fraternal twins (twins who do not have identical DNA) of homosexual men were gay. This result suggests strongly that while sexual orientation is not genetically fixed, it is at least foreshadowed in one's genetic code.

Scientists have put forth a number of theories to explain why a genetic bias might be expressed differently between twins. They largely agree that although there may be a genetic predisposition to homosexuality, this trait will not be expressed without an environmental push. The nature of the push is not known and could be almost anything. In a recent article, a geneticist who is studying this question explains his methods. "For each pair [of twins] we expect to see a whole lot of things that are random," he says. "Basically we compare the gay results with the straight ones and see if any [factor] shows up multiple times for these subjects."[12]

As of yet, no solid answers to this question have emerged. But twin studies are the scientific gold standard for determining a trait's heritability, so this line of research may well yield new clues in the future.

The On/Off Switch

Many scientists believe that a line of study called epigenetics is the key to understanding sexual orientation in identical twins and many other aspects of sexual orientation development. The idea behind epigenetics is that although a person's genes may be set in stone, the way those genes behave is not. Certain genes are susceptible to being turned on or off by environmental factors, including diet, lifestyle choices, behavior, stress, exposure to toxins, and countless other things. The changes caused by these factors are much too numerous and random to predict—and as scientist Simon LeVay points out, that is part of nature's design. Random variations are a necessary ingredient in human diversity. As he explains,

When we consider that mammals, including humans, possess only 20,000 genes or so, and that these genes have to regulate the development of billions of brain cells and all their synaptic connections, along with the entire remainder of the body, it's obvious that brain organization cannot be genetically specified in precise detail. Rather, genetic instructions produce trends and tendencies that allow for some diversity in outcome.[13]

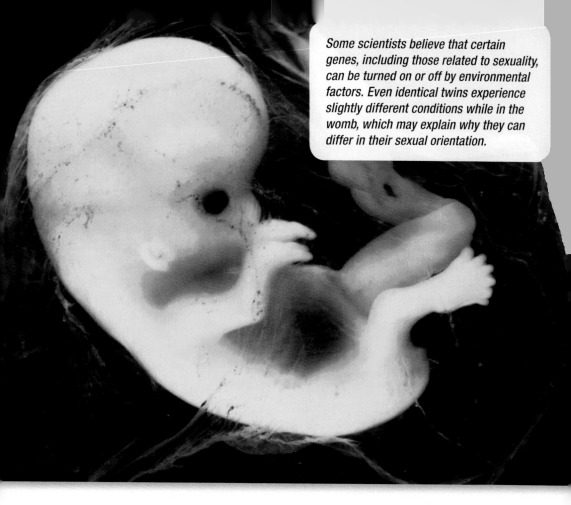

Some scientists believe that certain genes, including those related to sexuality, can be turned on or off by environmental factors. Even identical twins experience slightly different conditions while in the womb, which may explain why they can differ in their sexual orientation.

This diversity in outcome exists even in the womb, and this fact has attracted a great deal of attention from scientists interested in the question of sexual orientation. It has been pointed out that even identical twins experience slightly different conditions before birth—for example, one twin might be positioned higher in the womb or might receive more or less blood flow than the other twin. It is entirely possible that these types of differences could change the expression of some of a fetus's genes, including those related to sexuality, and this might explain why identical twins can differ in their sexual orientation.

Prenatal Hormones

The level of prenatal hormones a fetus receives is another environmental factor that varies from one mother and one pregnancy to another. It is well understood that certain hormones, including

Cultural Links to Homosexuality

In the search for the roots of sexual orientation, scientists have uncovered some interesting links between homosexuality and various cultural factors:

- **City life.** Surveys show that nonheterosexual populations are highly concentrated in urban areas. This concentration is partly because gay people gravitate to cities, but that does not seem to be the only reason. Studies also show that people born and raised in cities are more likely to be LGBTQ+ than those raised in more rural areas. Some scientists speculate that cities provide more opportunities for people to explore a gay lifestyle and eventually adopt this sexual orientation—a classic environmental argument.

- **Higher education.** College professors, as a group, are disproportionately likely to be homosexual. Psychologists suggest that the academic lifestyle appeals to gay populations because it requires both task independence and social perceptiveness, two qualities that many LGBTQ+ individuals acquire through life as a social minority.

- **Intelligence.** Several studies have found that high intelligence in childhood is associated with an increased likelihood of being gay in adulthood. This finding is fairly recent and is under continuing investigation.

testosterone and estrogen, help to drive a fetus's physical sexual development. Since the early 1900s, scientists have questioned whether these hormones might affect a fetus's future sexual orientation as well.

Studies of animals provide a great deal of evidence for this idea. Experiments have shown that male mouse and rat fetuses that receive lower-than-usual amounts of masculinizing hormones called androgens behave like females after birth, and they are likely to pursue other males as sex partners. Likewise, female mouse and rat fetuses that receive higher-than-usual amounts of androgens behave like males after birth, and they often show a sexual preference for other females. These changes in sexual orientation are often accompanied by physical changes, such as differences in the size of the sex organs or certain parts of the brain.

Similar studies cannot be done ethically with human beings, but scientists have discovered an ingenious way to retroactively measure fetal hormone levels in women at least. They have learned that the relative length of the second and fourth fingers on a woman's right hand is affected by prenatal androgens. In most adult women, the second finger is about the same length as the fourth finger, or sometimes just slightly shorter. In men, the pattern is different: The fourth finger is usually considerably longer than the second. By measuring and studying hundreds of human hands, researchers have discovered that the fingers of homosexual women, on average, have an unusually masculine ratio—the fourth fingers tend to be much longer than the second fingers. "This suggests that at least some lesbians were exposed to greater levels of fetal androgen than heterosexual women,"[14] the authors of one study concluded.

Gender-atypical development in the brain provides a similar piece of evidence. Scientists have long known that male and female brains have characteristic differences—for instance, some parts are larger in men than women, and vice versa. Recent studies have examined both cadaver brains and magnetic resonance imaging pictures of live brains. The researchers responsible for the studies claim to have uncovered certain female features in the brains of male homosexuals and male features in the brains of female homosexuals. These differences, they claim, would have been caused by prenatal hormone levels. This finding is the subject of much debate since the studies' sample sizes (the number of participants) were small, which leads some scientists to question whether the results are valid. But valid or not, the results are certainly interesting and will pave the way for further study.

> **WORDS IN CONTEXT**
>
> **androgens**
> Hormones, such as testosterone and androsterone, that promote the development of male sexual characteristics.

Fraternal Birth Order

An apparent correlation called the fraternal birth order effect is yet another piece of evidence supporting a biological basis for homosexuality. First proposed in the mid-1900s, this theory states that the more older brothers a man has from the same mother, the more likely that man is to be homosexual. Studies have shown repeatedly that each older brother increases a man's chance of being gay by anywhere between 28 and 48 percent.

The fraternal birth order effect is interesting in large part because it is so robust. In scientific terms, this means the result can be replicated over and over, throughout many different groups of subjects. It holds up across races, cultures, and time periods. Additionally, studies consistently show that the finding applies only to biological brothers and not to adopted siblings or step-brothers—and it only applies to men, not women. Between all of these factors, the effect is considered the strongest biological predictor of sexual orientation in men.

Although the fraternal birth order effect is now well established in scientific literature, it is not well understood. Some researchers suggest that it is the result of an immune response—in other words, carrying a male fetus causes certain changes in the mother's immune system that affect subsequent pregnancies. Whether or not this is the case, researchers do know that homosexuality linked to birth order is also related to birth weight and left- or right-handedness, physical traits that are known to be prenatally determined. This evidence provides strong support for the idea that sexual orientation is at least partially influenced in the womb.

But even scientists who wholeheartedly support this hypothesis are quick to point out that prenatal hormones do not tell the whole story. "There are plenty of gay men who are first-borns, many straight men with older brothers, and many women whose fingers give no clue to their sexual orientation," cautions Marc Breedlove, the scientist who discovered the finger-length correlation. "This is not a test to be used on your friends and neighbors."[15]

Early Childhood Environment

All of the genetic and environmental factors discussed up to this point occur in the womb, before a child is born. There is a great deal of scientific debate about whether the story ends here—in other words, whether sexual orientation is fixed at birth—or whether a child's postnatal environment also has an effect. Many studies have tried to answer this question. None has found any definitive results, but some interesting ideas have shown up that are much debated in scientific literature.

One such correlation, dubbed the exotic-becomes-erotic effect, is similar in concept to epigenetics. This theory states that some infants, although not exactly born homosexual, are genetically predisposed to certain behaviors that are not typical of their gender. As these babies grow into toddlers and then young children, they become increasingly aware that they are different from others of their own sex. This perception of difference—of being exotic—turns on the tendency toward homosexuality and leads the child to develop same-sex erotic feelings. These feelings increase as the child matures and eventually become hardwired into the person's core identity.

Some psychologists question whether parenting styles also might affect a child's eventual sexual orientation. Interviews of adult homosexual men show that in many cases, the men remember their fathers being hostile and distant and their mothers being overbearing and overprotective. This parenting atmosphere, says

Some psychologists question whether parenting style, such as that of a hostile father or an overbearing mother, may affect a child's eventual sexual orientation. However, the role of parental influence is a controversial topic that is not well supported by scientific studies.

the theory, leaves the child without a strong male role model and leads to homosexual tendencies, which become cemented over time.

The role of parental influence is a very controversial topic that is not well supported by scientific studies. Critics are concerned that this idea only attempts to explain homosexuality in men, not women, and they point out that childhood memories are notoriously inaccurate. They further say that even if a man's assessment of his childhood situation is completely correct, the lines of causation are unclear: did the father's hostility cause the son to become gay, or did the father become hostile because the son was acting in gender-atypical ways?

Despite these criticisms, parenting styles continue to come under scrutiny as a possible contributing factor to sexual orientation. It will be difficult for anyone to prove how or even if this process works. But parents undeniably do influence their children in myriad ways, and there is no compelling reason to exclude sexual orientation from consideration.

Formative Events

A home environment is a passive type of influence that surrounds and naturally sways a child. It is not a single event that happens to a person. Some scientists feel that it is more productive to look at specific childhood events rather than the overall environment when searching for the roots of sexual orientation.

A person's earliest sexual experience is one event that has been examined as a possible determinant of sexual orientation. According to this line of thinking, explains one scientist, "If a person's first sexual contact is with a woman, he or she will desire further contacts with women; if it is with a man, he or she will desire further contacts with men. Thus a person who starts off with no particular preference in sex partners gradually develops an ingrained attraction to one sex or the other."[16]

> **WORDS IN CONTEXT**
>
> **determinant**
> A factor that decisively affects the nature or outcome of something.

Homosexuality in Animals

In an attempt to understand the origins of human homosexuality, scientists have turned their eyes to the animal kingdom. They have discovered that homosexual behavior among animals does not just exist—it abounds. Same-sex dalliance has been recorded in about fifteen hundred species and is even more common than heterosexual activity in some populations.

Apes called bonobos are of particular interest to scientists because these animals are closely related to humans. Bonobos have so much sex that this pastime is jokingly called the bonobo handshake. An estimated 60 percent of this activity occurs between females, but same-sex contact also occurs between males, particularly as a way to make up after fighting. Individual bonobos are not fixed in their sexual habits; they will happily engage with same-sex and opposite-sex partners in rapid succession, showing little preference in the matter.

Many other species commonly engage in same-sex contact, including bottlenose dolphins, giraffes, macaques, and even fruit flies. About 8 percent of male domestic rams are exclusively homosexual, but this fixed preference is by far the exception, not the rule.

Animals do not have the intellectual capacity to make choices about their behavior; they just do what comes naturally. People, on the other hand, do have the ability to think, reason, and make informed choices. Exactly how—or whether—this ability relates to sexual orientation is an open question, and one that will undoubtedly continue to generate scientific debate over many years to come.

Studies do show that both gay men and lesbians are more likely than heterosexuals to have had same-sex contact with an older person during childhood or adolescence. At first glance, this fact seems to support the sexual experience theory. But opponents of this idea have pointed out many holes in the theory, particularly the fact that most people understand their sexual preferences before they have any sexual contact of any kind. Therefore, early sexual experiences might have an effect in some cases, but they cannot be wholly responsible for everyone's sexual orientation.

Childhood physical or sexual abuse is another type of event that has been studied for possible links to adult sexual orientation. It has been shown conclusively that gay men and lesbians report more childhood abuse than heterosexual people. Whether this abuse leads directly to homosexuality, however, is a different question. Some scientists think that this is, indeed, the case. But others suggest that non-gender-conforming children may attract the attention of potential abusers and are thus more likely to become targets. It is a chicken-and-egg question that, like so many others in the field of sexual orientation, is difficult to answer one way or the other.

Accepted or Not

The biggest chicken-and-egg question of all may concern the role of society itself. A study of human history shows that homosexuality is more common at times and in places where it is well accepted. Does an accepting atmosphere cause homosexuality, or does it simply allow people to express feelings that would stay buried under other circumstances? This question is complicated, and it is one that science may never be able to answer—although more clues will undoubtedly be uncovered as time goes by. With each discovery, psychologists will come a little bit closer to understanding the unique balance of genetics and environment that determines each person's sexual orientation.

CHAPTER 3

Forming a Sexual Identity

On an LGBTQ+ Internet discussion site, a woman discusses her struggles to understand her sexuality. "I'm still having trouble finding myself," she confesses. "I'm afraid of society and my family members, because I do not know what I am. My sister always jokes around saying that 'I'm GAY AND I SHOULD JUST ADMIT IT!' [but] I truly don't know."[17]

For openly gay television news reporter Anderson Cooper, the situation is just the opposite: he says he has always understood this aspect of himself. "I've always known I was gay from the time I was a little kid—I can't remember a time when I wasn't aware of it, even before I knew what it was or the name of it," he said in a 2013 interview. "Being gay is a blessing—I couldn't be more proud."[18]

Yet another person expresses a third reality. She says she does not really understand her sexuality, but she does not care. She is willing to let life unfold and explore her feelings along the way. "All I know is that I don't wanna label myself," she says. "I don't care what gender is standing in front of me. As long as I like the person and feel like I could be with that person, then that is good enough for me."[19]

All three of these people are expressing thoughts and feelings about their sexual identities. In psychological terms, sexual identity refers to a person's sense of himself or herself as a sexual being. It encompasses values, beliefs, roles, and behaviors.

Unlike sexual orientation, which is at least partly inborn, sexual identity is something a person develops over time in response to many different factors. Sexual feelings are the springboard, but

Television news reporter Anderson Cooper (pictured here) has known he was gay from the time he was a young child. Many people, however, struggle to understand their true sexual identity.

they merely kick off the process. A person's culture, environment, family, religion, and many other factors also come into play. Reconciling all of these factors is a task that is quick and easy for some people but lengthy and difficult for others. Yet regardless of how long it takes—or if, indeed, it is ever fully completed—the process of forming a sexual identity includes many well-recognized psychological steps and milestones.

Early Gender Conformity

The earliest clue to a child's sexual orientation, and thus his or her likely future sexual identity, comes from gender-related behavior. In psychological literature, this personality aspect is referred to as gender conformity. Children who behave in ways typical of their biological gender are said to show high gender conformity. Children who act more like the opposite sex are said to show gender nonconformity. These differences usually emerge by preschool age and may be evident as early as age two.

Gender nonconformity has been the subject of many scientific studies. Research has turned up a number of traits often seen in nonconforming children, including cross-gender clothing and grooming preferences; a preference for toys usually associated with the opposite sex; a preference for opposite-sex playmates; strong identification with opposite-sex characters in books, films, and television shows; a stated desire to be a member of the opposite sex; and refusal to accept one's biological gender (for instance, when told he is a boy, a biologically male child invariably replies, "No, I am a girl").

There are two ways to study childhood gender nonconformity. Retrospective studies question adult participants about their childhood memories and experiences, then analyze these answers for links and trends. Prospective studies rank a group of children according to their gender-related behavior, then follow these children into adulthood to see how they develop. Both types of studies have their strengths and weaknesses, but in regard to sexual identity, they are consistent in their results: they find that strongly gender-conforming children are very likely to become heterosexual adults, and strongly nonconforming children have a much higher-than-usual chance of forming a nonheterosexual identity. This correlation is more pronounced in men than in women, but it holds true for both sexes. In many cases, then, gender conformity or the lack thereof can be seen as the first stage in a child's sexual development.

> **WORDS IN CONTEXT**
>
> **gender conformity**
> The degree to which a person behaves in ways typical of his or her biological gender.

Feeling Different

At some point, non-gender-conforming children start to realize that they are different from their peers in terms of their behavior, their developing sexual feelings and interests, or both. Nonheterosexual

35

men, looking back at their youth, remember this phase starting at the average age of ten. For women it begins slightly later, around age eleven.

Some psychologists refer to this developmental period as the sensitization phase. Others call it the awareness phase. Whatever the label, this stage may last many years, and the young people who are going through it generally lack the life experience to understand their feelings. This time can therefore be very confusing, isolating, and frightening, although exciting as well. One adult lesbian's account of her sensitization period beautifully captures all of these feelings:

> Before I realized I found the girls around me attractive, I noticed their hair, the way they smelled. I exchanged clothes with them so that I could wear the way they smelled. I watched the way they moved. My heart pounded when they smiled at me, or talked to me, or invited me to do anything. . . . It was the exquisite awareness of their bodies near me. It was being hot and cold and flushed all over because my best friend was putting on lotion and I could see the fine hairs on her leg standing up in the cool room. All of this happened before I hit puberty, and long before I figured out there was anything sexual to it. I was simply achingly aware of them and I had no idea why.[20]

Identity Confusion

As time passes and a child's sexual feelings become more powerful, a new phase begins, usually around puberty. This phase is sometimes referred to as identity confusion. It is characterized by the conscious realization that one's thoughts, feelings, and behavior differ from society's heterosexual norms, and this realization leads to intense self-questioning about one's sexual identity.

This type of questioning can go on for a long time, and it may come and go from one period to another. One man describes the process in colorful terms: "It's like looking through the windshield on a rainy day. The wipers make a swipe, you see clearly for a moment, and then it hazes over, until the next wiper swipe. With each swipe, you see clearly, but in between, you convince yourself that

Roadblocks to Sexual Identity Development

Developing a sexual identity is a process that must take many outside factors into account. Here are some of the most common roadblocks for those who identify as homosexual:

- **Family rejection.** Parents make their viewpoints on countless subjects clear to their children, even without always meaning to. If parents are strongly homophobic (fearful of or angry toward homosexuals), their children may hesitate to be honest about their same-sex feelings.

- **Religious disapproval.** Many religious traditions are strongly opposed to homosexuality. These views may be taught to adherents from an early age, and some people believe them deeply and passionately. A church member who feels same-sex attraction may be very reluctant to admit these feelings, even to himself or herself, much less to the world at large.

- **Cultural backlash.** In some cultures, homosexuality is strictly forbidden and may even be illegal. The fear of this consequence is a strong deterrent to same-sex contact or even questioning oneself about it.

- **Social pressure.** Studies show that homosexual youth are bullied more frequently and more violently than almost any other social group. As adults, too, homosexuals are subjected to various negative societal pressures, including job and housing discrimination, refusal of health care services, and general interpersonal nastiness and ridicule. Some people would rather stay in the closet than deal with these daily obstacles.

what you saw must not have really been there,"[21] he says of his identity confusion period.

For most people the metaphorical rain clears at some point, and a better understanding of one's sexuality starts to emerge. This phase can come on quite suddenly, and it can be overwhelming. One gay man recalls this moment in vivid detail. Around age thirteen or fourteen, he was watching a movie and daydreaming in explicit terms about the lead male actor when suddenly it struck him: "I WAS GAY! . . . I had never had a rational thought about it. I had never said it in my mind. I had never comprehended the full meaning of the words. . . . I remember having some really bad anxiety which felt like a panic attack. I was covered in sweat, my heart was beating fast and my vision went black."[22]

Although many LGBTQ+ people recall a sharp moment of realization like this one, others report a more gradual process. It is common for people to spend years asking themselves questions like, "Am I really gay, or could I be bisexual?" "Will these feelings pass?" "Could I be straight, but feel attracted only to this one particular person of the same gender?" Some people never find the answers. But with time and experience, many people start to feel more and more certain of their sexual identity.

From Tolerance to Acceptance

The identity confusion phase ends when a person fully and consciously realizes that he or she is probably not heterosexual. Some people are immediately fine with this idea. Many others, however, are not. They enter a tolerance phase where they know the truth about themselves but are not yet happy or comfortable with it.

This phase is characterized by a slow shift in a person's social circles and behavior. The newly aware LGBTQ+ person starts to seek contact with like-minded people, sometimes in very discreet ways, such as on Internet message boards. He or she may feel increasingly uncomfortable in heterosexual groups and may shy away from previous friends.

As time passes and contact with the LGBTQ+ community increases, many people start to shift to more solid ground, emotionally and psychologically. They find support and acceptance from their new contacts, and they become increasingly comfortable with the idea of being gay. Some may also start to experiment with same-sex contact.

This social and sexual experimentation progresses until it reaches a tipping point, and the person begins to truly accept his

Once people realize that they are probably not heterosexual, they enter a tolerance phase that is characterized by a change in their social circles. They may seek contact with like-minded people in discreet ways, such as on Internet message boards, and may feel increasingly uncomfortable in heterosexual groups.

or her LGBTQ+ identity. Unlike the initial recognition of one's core differences from societal norms, which is often frightening, the acceptance phase is usually described as a positive step that is accompanied by feelings of enormous relief. "The whole thing is like you've been in a dark cage your whole life and somebody has released you out into the bright openness,"[23] said one woman after fully accepting her lesbian identity.

The Commitment Phase

Following the acceptance phase, many LGBTQ+ people enter a period that psychologists call the commitment phase. During this phase, the person embraces the idea that being nonheterosexual

Pride on Display

In 1976 a gay artist and drag queen named Gilbert Baker began to think about creating a symbol for the LGBTQ+ community. He felt that a flag would be the best format because flags represent nations. "We are a people, a tribe if you will. And flags are about proclaiming power, so it's very appropriate," he explained. "[But] we needed something *beautiful*, something from *us*."

Baker eventually hit on the rainbow as the ideal symbol. "The rainbow is so perfect because it really fits our diversity in terms of race, gender, ages, all of those things. Plus, it's a natural flag—it's from the sky!" he said. Baker's original rainbow had eight horizontal stripes of different colors. Over the years the design was refined to the current version, which has six stripes: red, orange, yellow, blue, green, and violet.

Today Baker's rainbow is an internationally recognized symbol of LGBTQ+ solidarity. No longer restricted to flags, it adorns every imaginable item, from clothing to cell phone cases, jewelry to car license plates, and everything in between. Displayed proudly and frequently in most population centers, it reminds people struggling with sexual identity issues that they are not alone—and that a vibrant community awaits them with open arms.

Quoted in Paola Antonelli, "MoMA Acquires the Rainbow Flag," Museum of Modern Art, June 17, 2015. www .moma.org.

is a valid and satisfying self-image and starts to incorporate this idea into his or her core personality. This does not necessarily mean that a person is ready to go public with his or her sexual identity; in fact, the early stages of the commitment phase can be internal and very private. "I can't say that I immediately came out . . . but I at least came out to myself," says one man who recalls being very circumspect about his sexuality as a teenager, even after accepting his homosexuality. "I knew I was gay and didn't pretend to be anything but gay inside my own head. No matter what the world thought, I at least knew who I was."[24]

For most LGBTQ+ people, this need for perfect privacy passes with time, and the feeling of commitment to a nonheterosexual identity starts creeping into their behavior and life choices. It is common in this phase for people to start presenting themselves in stereotypically gay ways—for instance, a lesbian might get a masculine haircut and start wearing plaid shirts and combat boots, or a gay man might adopt a more feminine style of speaking. Although these people are not necessarily public about their sexuality yet, they are becoming less afraid of being judged and more willing to push social boundaries.

> **WORDS IN CONTEXT**
>
> **commitment**
> A developmental stage during which a person embraces the idea that being LGBTQ+ is a valid and satisfying self-image and starts to incorporate this belief into his or her life and actions.

A major step in the commitment phase occurs when a person enters a lasting romantic relationship that falls outside the heterosexual norms in any way. This is a psychological milestone because the person can no longer claim to be just experimenting with his or her sexuality. He or she is making a lifestyle choice that has long-lasting emotional, sexual, and practical repercussions. By doing so, the LGBTQ+ person reaches a new depth of commitment to his or her sexual identity.

Coming Out

When this commitment level reaches a psychological point of no return, many LGTBQ+ people feel that it is no longer practical or

A group of women pose for a photo during the 24th Annual Dyke March in New York City. For LGBTQ+ people, choosing to come out, or tell others about their sexual orientation, can be liberating as well as frightening.

desirable to keep their true selves hidden, and they start telling people about their sexual orientation. Doing this is called *coming out*. This term is short for *coming out of the closet*, a phrase that suggests that gay people who keep their sexual orientation private are shut away in a small, restrictive psychological box. By leaving this closet, these people are choosing a larger life with more options and much more emotional honesty.

Although coming out is liberating, it can also be frightening. People do not always know how their friends, families, and the world at large will react to their announcement. They may fear being rejected by their loved ones, their churches, their bosses and colleagues, or any number of other people who may disapprove of nonheterosexual lifestyles—and this can, indeed, be the case. For this reason most LGBTQ+ organizations recommend a careful and well-considered approach to coming out.

With just a little caution, however, it is possible to navigate the coming-out process with chiefly positive results. LGBTQ+ people overwhelmingly report that their fears turned out to be unjustified and that most people were supportive of their sexual orientation—sometimes surprisingly so. "My older sister . . . I think found more excitement in my being gay than I ever did," chuckles one woman who came out as a lesbian when she was a teenager. "The prospect of gay pride parades and rainbow stickers just filled her with joy. To this day I think she has attended more gay events than I ever have."[25]

The results are not always this positive, of course. But even LBGTQ+ people who have encountered negative reactions say they are glad to be out. One young Turkish Muslim man, whose culture frowns upon homosexuality, reports that he was shunned by his parents and lost most of his old friends after coming out as gay—but despite these negative outcomes, he is content with his decision. "Coming out, and encouraging others to do so, has given my life meaning," he says on an Internet message board. "Being open, honest, has given me freedom. I've never been this happy in my whole life."[26]

The Transgender Path

For cisgender people, even those who identify as gay, the path to defining sexual identity is fairly straightforward and well understood. The process is more complicated for transgender people, who must sort through issues of gender identity as well. This issue was addressed by Caitlyn Jenner, arguably the world's most famous transgender person, in a 2015 interview. Formerly known as Bruce Jenner, an Olympic athlete and the patriarch of the Kardashian/Jenner clan, Jenner had recently come out as transgender. When asked, "Are you a lesbian?" Jenner replied, "You're going back to the sex thing, and it's apples and oranges. Sexuality is who you are personally attracted to. But gender identity is who you are as a person and your soul and who you identify as inside." Jenner goes on to explain that although she lives and sees herself as a woman, she is still attracted to other women: "No, I'm not gay. I am, as far as I know, heterosexual. I've never been with a guy, I've always been married, raising kids."[27]

At a glance, these words are easy to take at face value. But a deeper examination raises difficult questions. For instance, Jenner sees herself as a woman, with an attraction to other women, but identifies as heterosexual instead of lesbian. Meanwhile, Laverne Cox, a famous transgender actress from the television show *Orange Is the New Black*, is not forthcoming about her sexual identity—but in sharp contrast to Jenner, she is open about the fact that she prefers men. Whatever words Cox may choose to define her sexual identity, she has had to balance gender and orientation—as have all other transgender people—to arrive at her final self-image.

A Lifelong Journey

Laying out the steps of sexual identity development in a clear, sequential way, as this chapter has done, is somewhat misleading. Although this psychological journey does sometimes proceed in an orderly manner, this is not always the case. People can go back and forth between various stages, progress quickly or slowly, or tackle several stages at once. They can also reach a certain stage of the process and then freeze there, making little to no progress throughout the rest of their lives.

For those who complete the journey, though, the rewards are immense. Sexuality is an important part of each person's psychological makeup. By arriving at a healthy, comfortable sexual identity—whatever that identity may be—a person can live in ways that are true to his or her authentic inner self.

CHAPTER 4

Life as an LGBTQ+ Person

A gay man who goes by the online handle C.G. has been open about his sexuality for a long time. He has completely accepted his sexual identity and the lifestyle that accompanies it. He has even assumed a leadership role in the gay community, working with nonheterosexual youth to help them cope with the issues and struggles they are facing. Yet as comfortable as he is, C.G. admits that he has mixed feelings about his path in life. "Sometimes I still struggle with the fact that people can't accept me for being gay. But at the same time, I love being gay and I love my friends and the people who do care about me. I try to ignore those who don't support me but I know it's hard,"[28] he says.

These comments capture a core truth about life as an LGBTQ+ person: it is not always easy. Nonheterosexual people are a minority in society, and like most minorities, they tend to be misunderstood. This misunderstanding leads to an elevated incidence of interpersonal prejudice and discrimination. One unpleasant incident might not have much impact, but repeated episodes over time can become increasingly difficult to deal with. And even if a person does not experience any overt discrimination, he or she may feel a subtle, constant thrum of disapproval and invalidation from the heterosexual majority. This undercurrent may be unspoken, but it can be exhausting and discouraging nonetheless.

As if this were not difficult enough, nonheterosexual individuals also face unique pressures that come from within the LGBTQ+ community and also from themselves. Combined, all of these things create a burden that some people handle well—but many others do not. Over decades of working with this group, scientists have come to recognize many psychological trends and pressures that affect the LGBTQ+ community.

Internalized Homophobia

The most basic type of psychological pressure comes from within. Most nonheterosexual people struggle to some degree with an issue psychologists call internalized homophobia, which is self-hatred related to sexual identity. From their earliest days—long before they are sexually aware—children perceive and absorb society's negative messages about homosexuality. When they get older and start to question their sexual identity, they start to apply these negative messages to themselves.

One gay man describes his personal struggle with internalized homophobia in eloquent terms. "You're impressionable when you're young. When I came to terms with my sexuality, I was trying to accept who I was," he says. "But I still had all these notions I'd been taught while growing up. It's easy to put aside those prejudices and acknowledge that that's all they are—but still, there's this lingering default feeling that sticks around. You can't just put that aside."[29]

Internalized homophobia manifests in different ways from one person to another. For some people, it is a minor annoyance that pops up occasionally as a self-deprecating thought, quickly and easily dismissed. For others, it is a driving force—although often subconscious—that affects many aspects of life. Buried feelings of self-hatred can lead to countless negative outcomes and behaviors, including low self-esteem, poor school and work performance, avoidance of anything considered gay for fear of what others might think, bullying or ridiculing other LGBTQ+ people, self-destructive actions and habits, and much more.

> **WORDS IN CONTEXT**
>
> **internalized homophobia**
> Self-hatred that arises when LGBTQ+ people absorb society's negativity about homosexuality and apply it to themselves.

Gaydar

The popular term *gaydar* describes the ability to guess someone's sexual identity by evaluating his or her looks, behavior, voice, dress, and other outward attributes. There has been considerable debate over whether this ability really exists, with some scientific studies confirming it and others debunking it. One of the most recent studies in the field, however, suggests strongly that gaydar is real.

The study in question showed a series of black-and-white facial photographs to college students. Each photo appeared for just fifty milliseconds—less time than it takes to blink one's eyes. The photos were digitally altered to remove hair, jewelry, and other "self-presentational" aspects of each person. Even with these changes, students were able to correctly guess the photographic subjects' sexual orientation 57 percent of the time, on average—a much higher-than-expected number. Some respondents did even better, scoring above 80 percent accuracy on the task.

Researcher Joshua Tabak believes that this proficiency develops through exposure to a wide variety of gay and straight people, and it is probably highest among sexually diverse populations (such as the college students who participated in this study). He also suggests that in a real-world situation, where hair, jewelry, clothing, gait, and posture are added to the mix, people's gaydar might well be even better. But perhaps most important, he says, is the speed at which it happens. "It's judged so rapidly and efficiently, it suggests that we may actually be judging sexual orientation without intending to in everyday life," he says.

Jason Koebler, "Study Finds 'Gaydar' Up to 80 Percent Accurate on Sexuality," *U.S. News & World Report*, May 12, 2012. www.usnews.com.

The first step in dealing with internalized homophobia is recognizing it. Once a person admits to having these thoughts and feelings, he or she can work to reduce or eliminate them through counseling, self-affirmation, or other positive processes. These efforts, in turn, can lead to a healthier, more positive self-image.

Reconciling Religious Beliefs

For religious individuals, the job of conquering internalized homophobia can be especially difficult. In certain religious traditions, homosexuality is considered sinful and wrong. People who have grown up believing these teachings, but who eventually feel the stirrings of same-sex attraction, often find it difficult to reconcile these disparate parts of their personality.

A woman named Sonia who grew up in a strongly religious community remembers how painful this process was for her. When Sonia first realized she was a lesbian, she recalls,

> I took out my student Bible and searched for hours on homosexuality. . . . There were a couple of passages that I thought were scolding me. They told me I was evil and hateful, that my kind is unforgiven and will forever burn. It was the harshest thing I had ever read. I probably prayed more within that week than I had ever prayed in my life. I begged for God to tell me if I was wrong and evil. I cried to myself, trying to get myself to believe that I'm not what they say I am. It took me a while to pull through that.[30]

Sonia's story has a happy ending. She did eventually find a balance between her religion and her sexual identity, and many other LGBTQ+ individuals have navigated these tricky waters as well. The path is not always easy and may involve significant changes in an individual's life, such as removing oneself from strongly negative people, switching to a church that welcomes gays, or even abandoning formal religion altogether and forging a private spiritual path. With an open mind and attitude, however, it is very possible for LGBTQ+ people to enjoy a robust religious life while staying true to their authentic inner selves.

Pressure from Society

Although religious disapproval is a strong factor for only some LGBTQ+ people, pressures of different types affect the entire gay community. LGBTQ+ people face negative attitudes, behaviors, and actions from many of the people and organizations around them every day.

In the United States, an organization called GLSEN (pronounced "Glisten") has been monitoring some of these pressures

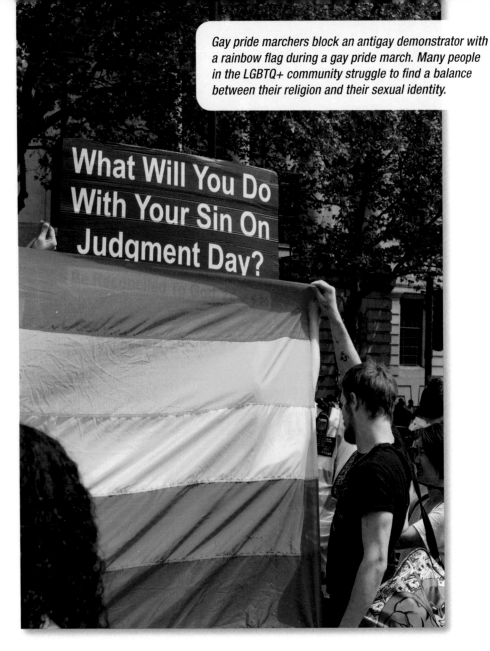

Gay pride marchers block an antigay demonstrator with a rainbow flag during a gay pride march. Many people in the LGBTQ+ community struggle to find a balance between their religion and their sexual identity.

What Will You Do With Your Sin On Judgment Day?

since 1990. GLSEN was founded to combat discrimination, harassment, and bullying based on sexual orientation, gender identity, and gender expression in primary through secondary schools. Every two years the organization releases a report called the National School Climate Survey that compiles input from thousands of LGBTQ+ students all over the country. The most recent survey, which came out in 2015, lists a number of alarming statistics. It states, among other things, that 98.1 percent of gay students reported hearing homophobic remarks at school, both from other students and from teachers; 85.2 percent had been verbally abused by other students; 48.6 percent had been the victims of cyberbullying; and 40 percent had been physically harassed (pushed or shoved) or assaulted (punched, kicked, or injured with a weapon) because of their sexual orientation.

This type of school atmosphere has many negative consequences. According to GLSEN, more than half of all LGBTQ+ youth say they feel unsafe among their peers at school, especially in locker rooms and restrooms. Students also tend to feel that they cannot report homophobic incidents to school staff because the administration itself is often a source of discrimination—66.2 percent of respondents had personally experienced policies or practices at school that were discriminatory against LGBTQ+ students. As the combined result of all these pressures, gay and transgender students skip school more regularly than their heterosexual peers, earn lower grade point averages, tend to avoid extracurricular activities, and are much less likely to go on to college. Based on this information and other findings, GLSEN concludes, "It is clear that there is an urgent need for action to create safe and affirming learning environments for LGBTQ students."[31]

Mental Health Minefield

GLSEN's surveys are useful because they provide perhaps the most comprehensive snapshot of homophobia in America. However, they only describe the tip of the iceberg. After leaving school, LGBTQ+ people continue to encounter discrimination and prejudice due to their sexual orientation and/or gender expression. Due largely to this ongoing stress, the gay community is disproportionately prone to certain psychological problems.

Depression and anxiety are two such problems. According to the National Alliance on Mental Illness (NAMI), LGBTQ+ individuals are almost three times more likely than the general population to experience major depression or a generalized anxiety disorder. These people often do not seek help, says NAMI, because they distrust the medical community and society at large.

As a result, their mental health issues go untreated, which can lead to further problems, including substance abuse. An estimated 20 to 30 percent of the LGBTQ+ population abuse illegal drugs, alcohol, and/or tobacco, compared to 9 percent of the general population.

The tendency to self-harm is another problem that affects the LGBTQ+ community. NAMI states that homosexual people are about four times more likely to attempt suicide than their straight counterparts. Many other LGBTQ+ people have no intention of killing themselves, but they do things to harm themselves. "I began to hate myself when I gradually became more and more convinced about my sexuality, trying to cut myself with any sharp thing I could lay my hands on, knives, scissors, blades, anything at all," one gay man recalls when recounting his life story. "Whenever such thoughts came into my head, I went and locked myself in my room and tried to hurt myself."[32]

The discrimination and prejudice experienced by LGBTQ+ individuals makes them disproportionately prone to depression and anxiety. An estimated 20 to 30 percent of the LGBTQ+ population abuse illegal drugs, alcohol, and/or tobacco in an effort to combat their mental health issues.

Gender Dysphoria

Self-harming tendencies reach their peak in the transgender community, which is notoriously prone to depression. According to NAMI, over 65 percent of transgender people report that they think regularly about suicide—a thought pattern known as suicidal ideation.

This problem stems largely from a psychological disorder called gender dysphoria, which is defined as the distress a person feels due to his or her biological gender. This disorder is classified as a mental illness in the fifth edition of American Psychiatric Association's *Diagnostic and Statistical Manual of Mental Disorders,* although it carries the following disclaimer: "Gender nonconformity is not in itself a mental disorder. The critical element of gender dysphoria is the presence of clinically significant distress associated with the condition."[33]

The impact of gender dysphoria varies greatly from person to person, ranging from mild unhappiness to crippling misery. Whatever the degree, the cure involves bringing one's physical appearance into line with one's mental and emotional reality. Some transgender people feel satisfied dressing and grooming themselves in accordance with their gender identity. Others feel the need to alter their bodies through drugs, surgery, or a combination of the two. This approach is unquestionably drastic—but it can have life-changing psychological impacts. "I am just now getting to the point where when I look in the mirror who I see is more woman than man and that is super exciting!" exclaimed one person during her male-to-female physical transition. "There is this feeling of completeness and connectedness with my body that is slowly but surely creeping up on me. It is like nothing I have ever experienced."[34] For this woman, as for many others, physical change is the springboard to better mental health.

Dating and Sex

Once people leap the various mental health hurdles of an LGBTQ+ status, they can start settling into their new identity and lifestyle. They quickly find, however, that LGBTQ+ life comes with some unique challenges. Perhaps the most fundamental challenges involve dating and sex, which can be more complicated for gay and transgender people than they are for the heterosexual population.

One reason for this difficulty is purely a matter of numbers. There are far fewer people in the LGBTQ+ community than in the

Pride Parades

Feelings of gay pride and community reach their peak during pride parades, which occur in many cities and nations around the world. During these events, some members of the LGBTQ+ community march with their favorite organizations in parade units. Many other people, both gay and straight, line the streets to watch the show. They wave rainbow flags and cheer to celebrate diversity and acceptance for all people.

Pride parades generally offer a mixed bag of content. Some marchers are just out to have fun and to demonstrate the flamboyant style sometimes expressed in the LGBTQ+ community. Blasting music, dancing drag queens, and colorful floats create a high-energy, party-loving atmosphere. Other units take a more serious note, carrying signs or paraphernalia advertising gay-friendly organizations or touting political messages. Supportive churches, clubs, and other groups often march, as do memorial groups honoring victims of the AIDS epidemic and other tragedies that have touched the LGBTQ+ community.

The undisputed champion of the pride parade world is the São Paulo Gay Pride Parade in Brazil, which attracts an estimated 2.5 million people each year. Other million-plus parades occur in Madrid, Spain; San Francisco, California; London, England; Rome, Italy; and Cologne, Germany. At these events and countless others, the LGBTQ+ community can ignore homophobia, discrimination, and other societal pressures for a while and focus on the mutual support and respect that underlies all aspects of LGBTQ+ life.

heterosexual community, which means the pool of dating partners is much more limited. This can make it hard for nonheterosexual people to find desirable mates. "I know straight people struggle with relationships too, but they've got 95 percent of the population to play with," grumbles one gay man. "I've got a fraction of the remaining 5 percent—more likely 2 percent."[35]

Another difficulty goes back to societal pressure. Heterosexual couples typically do not get a second glance if they act affectionate in public, but homosexual couples often attract stares and glares. Some LGBTQ+ people do not mind this attention, but others find it very stressful, threatening, and unpleasant. Learning to handle it takes time and confidence, and the process can take a toll on a person's mental health and happiness.

Yet another issue involves sexual contact. LGBTQ+ youth in particular often point out that declaring a nonheterosexual identity is not the same thing as being ready for sex. In other words, a person may feel certain of his or her LGBTQ+ identity but feel too young or otherwise unready for sexual contact. Standing firm on this point can be a tricky balancing act for people who want the benefits of belonging to the LGBTQ+ community but do not yet want to embark upon a physical relationship.

Stereotypes vs. Authenticity

Avoiding dating and sex might solve some problems, but others remain. One common issue reported by many members of the LGBTQ+ community is intense pressure to conform to certain stereotypes and standards of behavior. Gay men, for instance, may feel that they are expected to dress well, speak in a slightly feminine manner, and worship musicians such as Cher, Madonna, and Barbra Streisand. Lesbians may feel pressured to dress and act more masculine than they feel. People who refuse to conform to these stereotypes and others sometimes feel like they do not fit in. "I feel a huge disconnect with gay culture," explains one man who holds this viewpoint. "For some the gay community and culture brings acceptance and community, but for me, I feel isolated because I know I don't belong."[36]

Members of the LGBTQ+ community often feel intense pressure to conform to specific stereotypes and standards of behavior. Gay men, for example, may feel that they are expected to dress well and worship certain musicians such as Cher or Madonna (pictured).

The solution to this problem, as it is to so many others, is to develop a strong self-image and find the courage to live authentically. For people who find support and comfort in conformity, stereotypes can provide a solid psychological base. Those who prefer a more individual approach will have more work to do. With patience and persistence, however, LGBTQ+ people of all types are usually able to find their comfort zone. As one lesbian puts it, "You don't need to 'live' or 'act' like a gay person. You're just a person, just like any other person. Be yourself and be happy. Don't change who you are based on what you think people want you to be."[37]

Creating Community

After reading to this point, it may seem that LGBTQ+ life is overwhelmingly difficult—and it would, indeed, be unfair to downplay the challenges faced by this group. They exist, and they are significant. But at the same time, it is important to recognize that there are many positive psychological aspects of the LGBTQ+ lifestyle.

Perhaps the most important such aspect is the strong sense of cohesion that unites the LGBTQ+ community. All gay and transgender people, regardless of their individual situations, face similar problems from society at large. This shared adversity often leads to a sense of camaraderie, accompanied by a passionate sense of belonging and mutual acceptance. "Being an out gay man creates instant networks," explains one person. "When moving, I can always join the GLB [gay, lesbian, bisexual] chorus and have an instant social group. Some places I can just walk down the street to a coffee shop where gay people hang out and find instant community."[38]

This community is not only about acceptance; it is also about support. Many people who have been happily, openly LGBTQ+ for a long time remember how hard things were in their younger days, when they were still struggling to come out. They are often willing and even eager to help newbies who are just starting on their journey to self-acceptance. These newcomers to the scene, in turn, will eventually be in a position to help others. "I've become very involved in organizing bi-related events," says one man who vividly remembers his early coming out days. "This is my way of paying back all those who I met and who supported me during my early days of finding my identity."[39]

The Key to Happiness

For this man and many others who feel the same way, giving back to the LGBTQ+ community is an important and satisfying part of their self-identity. For other people, the path to a psychologically healthy LGBTQ+ life may be different. All such journeys have their inherent challenges—but these challenges, as difficult as they may be, can bring great rewards. "The things that make being gay actually difficult only makes us work harder for what we deserve," points out one writer. "Our trials have made us resilient, thick-skinned, compassionate, and united. The truth is, we are winning."[40] By embracing and overcoming the challenges of this lifestyle, LGBTQ+ people can find not just happiness but significant personal growth as well.

CHAPTER 5

Can Sexual Identity and Orientation Be Changed?

In an online debate forum, an anonymous poster expressed the opinion that sexual orientation and identity are unchangeable. "There is no way to tell a person what their sexual orientation should be. They have something inside them that tells them what to feel and who to feel it for. This is inside them since birth," the person said. "It isn't possible to sway someone just because you don't like what they are choosing."[41]

In response, another person expressed very different ideas. "Everyone is born straight, because to be heterosexual is to follow the natural way of things. If someone is homosexual then something has happened to them to make them that way. And if someone is homosexual, it doesn't define them. They don't have to be homosexual. It is a choice,"[42] argued this poster.

These comments neatly sum up two sides of an extremely controversial question: can sexual orientation and identity be changed? Some people firmly believe that these things are a matter of choice and they not only can be changed but *should* be changed, if they differ from society's heterosexual norms. Others feel that sexual orientation and identity are a fixed part of a person's biology and personality, and any attempts to alter them—either through personal desire or outside intervention—are not only futile but also potentially harmful.

Opinions like these, of course, are no substitute for hard data. But on this particular question, scientists have not been able to provide a definitive answer. They have, however, uncovered many interesting clues. Historical analysis, modern scientific study, and anecdotal evidence all help to shed light on the changeability—or lack thereof—of sexual orientation and identity.

Variation Across Cultures

People who believe that sexual orientation and identity are changeable often cite historic and cross-cultural trends as evidence for their point of view. They point out that the incidence of homosexuality seems to vary from place to place and time to time, being quite common in some societies and virtually unknown in others. They believe this variation shows that homosexuality is a deliberate choice, made more frequently when it is socially acceptable.

Ancient Greece provides one example that supports this idea. Historical documents from this society show that homosexual relationships, particularly between older men and teenage boys, were not only accepted but also expected. Such relationships were actually a rite of passage for upper-class Athenian boys, who received patronage and guidance from their older lovers. Most of these boys went on to traditional male/female marriages as adults. Presumably most of them did, in fact, have an essentially heterosexual orientation but chose to engage in same-sex relationships for a short period of their lives.

In modern cultures, shifting levels of homosexuality seem to be related more to societal pressure than to choice. In America, for instance, homosexuality was considered unacceptable and was actually against the law until about the late 1960s, when attitudes began to change. Before this time, relatively few Americans would admit to being LGBTQ+. Today homosexuality is much more widely accepted, both legally and in popular opinion, and the American LGBTQ+ community has grown much larger as a result. The same trend is occurring around the world in other nations with tolerant attitudes and policies toward homosexuals.

The opposite is true in nations that take a more restrictive stance. Homosexuality is still illegal in dozens of countries around the world. As of 2016, it was even punishable by death in ten countries, including Yemen, Iran, Nigeria, Saudi Arabia, and others. Not surprisingly, open homosexuality is low to nonexistent in these nations.

Changing Medical Views

Published in 1952, the first *Diagnostic and Statistical Manual of Mental Disorders (DSM)* of the American Psychiatric Association (APA) listed homosexuality as a mental illness. The second edition of the manual, *DSM-II*, followed suit. In 1973, however, this entry was removed from the *DSM-III*, and it has remained absent from subsequent editions. This change was prompted by the newly emerged psychiatric consensus that homosexuality was not an illness but rather a normal variation of the human condition.

The APA's position has been extremely influential in the treatment of the LGBTQ+ community. Observers credit the normalization of homosexuality with many positive outcomes, including the following:

- The repeal of laws that criminalized homosexuality

- New laws protecting the rights of LGBTQ+ people in society and the workplace

- The ability of LGBTQ+ personnel to serve openly in the military

- Marriage equality and civil unions in many countries

- The legal right of LGBTQ+ people to adopt children

- Eased restrictions on gay spouses' right of inheritance

- An increased tolerance of gay parishioners and clergy in many religious denominations

The push behind these changes seems to center on the concept of normalcy. When homosexuality is considered normal rather than deviant, it is much harder to justify punishing or discriminating against LGBTQ+ individuals. By changing one small entry in a book, the APA changed the world for this community.

The great debate centers around the reason for these differences. Do people in restrictive societies weigh their options and decide that being gay is a bad choice, and consciously adopt a heterosexual identity instead—or do they hide their true feelings out of fear? On the flip side, do people in tolerant societies similarly weigh their options and consciously decide to take the LGBTQ+ route? There is no scientifically certain answer to this question.

However, data from multiple studies around the world suggest that the incidence of homosexuality is fairly consistent in any human population. If this is true, then the variation of homosexuality from one time and place to another is probably a matter of suppression, not true choice.

Same-Sex Environments

This is not to say, however, that homosexual behavior—which is not the same thing as having an LGBTQ+ identity—is never a choice. Heterosexual people can and often do choose to engage in same-sex contact when circumstances encourage it. They are particularly prone to do so in same-sex environments, such as prison, male- or female-only boarding schools, and single-sex military units.

In a 2015 study of sexual activity in the US penal system, one self-described heterosexual man described his experience.

Heterosexual people sometimes choose to engage in same-sex contact when circumstances encourage it. They are particularly prone to do so in same-sex environments, such as prison, male- or female-only boarding schools, and single-sex military units.

He said he had had consensual sex with gay and bisexual male prisoners "out of necessity," and added that he had been exclusively heterosexual since leaving prison. "I'm completely straight," he told the interviewer. "What happened then was just about having my sexual needs met, in a particular time and place, where I couldn't get [heterosexual] sex."[43]

WORDS IN CONTEXT

consensual
Engaged in by the mutual consent of all participants.

This man's story underscores once again the difference between sexual orientation, identity, and behavior. The man's sexual orientation and identity never changed; he remained firmly heterosexual in his core desires and self-image during his incarceration. His behavior, however, did change—and that was certainly a matter of choice. Had this man abstained from same-sex contact, that would also have been a choice. But neither choice, it should be noted, would necessarily have affected the man's innermost identity or desires.

Sexual Fluidity

The situation is different when it comes to sexual fluidity, a term that refers to changing sexual desires and orientation over time. This type of change occurs even without the pressures of a same-sex environment. A heterosexual man or woman in a long-term traditional marriage, for example, may unexpectedly fall in love with a same-sex partner, or a committed gay man or lesbian may discover an attraction to an opposite-sex partner. The person's sexual identity may change as a result. In other words, someone who previously thought of himself or herself as straight may re-identify as LGBTQ+, and someone who previously identified as homosexual may reidentify as straight.

This is not always the case, however. It is not uncommon for people to enter liaisons or relationships that depart from their usual preferences while keeping their basic self-concept intact. One researcher cites the case of Violet, a heterosexual woman who was shocked when she fell in love with a coworker named Susan. The two women enjoyed a twelve-year romantic and physical relationship. During and after the pairing, says the researcher, "Violet did not define herself as gay . . . nor has she become involved in another same-sex relationship since. Her 'sexual turnaround' applied to Susan and Susan alone."[44]

Psychological literature is full of examples like those cited above. It is obvious that people can and sometimes do change their sexual behavior, orientations, and identities over time. This

Sexual fluidity refers to changing sexual desires and orientation over time. For example, a heterosexual person in a traditional marriage may unexpectedly fall in love with a same-sex partner, and may change his or her sexual identity as a result.

fact has been used to support the idea that sexuality is a choice: if people *do* change—which they do, indisputably—then they *can* change. Whether or not they do so, the argument goes, is a matter of personal desire and willpower and has nothing to do with inborn, unchangeable qualities.

Other people disagree with this concept. They point out that self-knowledge can be tricky. Just because people have arrived at a certain sexual identity or orientation does not mean they fully understand or appreciate every corner of their sexuality. Sexual fluidity may therefore represent an emergence of feelings that were always there but perhaps were unrealized. The fact that people change, they say, is inevitable, uncontrollable, and definitely not a matter of conscious choice.

Unintentional Experiments

It would be difficult to design a scientific experiment to test these ideas of sexual fluidity. In addition, it definitely would be unethical to run such an experiment because tampering with a person's gender identity or sexual identity would likely cause a great deal of distress. However, scientists have been able to study a handful of unintentional experiments in which medical necessity forced a child's assigned sex to be switched soon after birth.

The best-known case began in 1966. It involved a child named Bruce Reimer, whose penis was destroyed in a botched circumcision at the age of seven months. Doctors advised Bruce's parents that since the baby had not yet developed a sexual or gender identity, the best course of action was to remove the testicles and raise him as a girl. Bruce's parents followed this advice. They renamed their son Brenda and treated him as a girl in all ways from that point forward.

If sexual orientation and gender identity were determined purely by one's environment, Brenda should have identified as a female in every respect. But this was not the case. Although

Brenda was not told she was a biological male, she knew she hated being a girl. When she got old enough, she also knew that she was sexually attracted to women, not men. She became more and more miserable until, at age fourteen, her parents finally told her the truth. Brenda immediately made the decision to transition back to male, renaming herself David. David eventually married a woman because his sexual orientation had remained solidly consistent with his biological sex, contrary to all medical and psychological expectations.

One case study, however, is not conclusive evidence. But Bruce/Brenda/David's story is not an isolated incident. A 1995

Lasting Harm

As a teen, a man named T.C. entered group conversion therapy at his parents' insistence. He recounted his experiences in a recent article:

> The first step—which usually lasted six months—[is] where they "deconstruct us as a person." Their tactics still haunt me. Aversion therapy, shock therapy, harassment and occasional physical abuse. Their goal was to get us to hate ourselves for being LGBTQ (most of us were gay, but the entire spectrum was represented), and they knew what they were doing. . . . The second step of the program, they "rebuilt us in their image." They removed us of everything that made us a unique person, and instead made us a walking, talking, robot for Jesus. They retaught us everything we knew. How to eat, talk, walk, dress, believe, even breathe. We were no longer people at the end of the program.

For T.C., as for most conversion therapy participants, these extreme efforts did not work. T.C. continued to identify as gay. He escaped from conversion therapy by feigning a complete "cure" to his family—a lie that he maintains to this day. He is openly gay in other areas of his life, although it took him many years and support from neutral counselors to undo the psychological damage he sustained during the conversion therapy process.

Quoted in James Michael Nichols, "A Survivor of Gay Conversion Therapy Shares His Chilling Story," *Huffington Post*, November 17, 2016. www.huffingtonpost.com.

study out of Johns Hopkins University looked at fourteen males who were reassigned as females soon after birth due to severe genital malformations. The study's authors discovered that most of these children chose to transition back to male at some point and were sexually attracted to women. A minority of the children did think of themselves as female—but they, too, were attracted to women, and they identified as lesbians. For these subjects, at least, sexual orientation seems to be firmly and irrevocably ingrained despite the most compelling reasons to change it.

Conversion Therapy

It is important to note the difference between sexual orientation and identity in the Johns Hopkins study. The sexual identities of some subjects changed; the sexual orientations did not. This study and many others suggest strongly that sexual orientation is difficult, if not impossible, to adjust.

Yet despite the growing body of evidence to support this idea, many people remain convinced that sexual orientation can, indeed, be changed, and a small but energetic industry—often affiliated with fundamentalist religious groups—exists to help in this effort. Attempts to change sexual orientation from homosexual to heterosexual are known collectively as conversion therapies, and they take many forms, including psychotherapy, behavior modification techniques, sex therapy sessions, prayer groups, and more. Some people seek these services willingly, wanting desperately to subdue their same-sex impulses and conform to society's heterosexual norm. Others, particularly teens, may be forced into conversion therapy by upset parents who cannot accept the idea of having an LGBTQ+ child.

> **WORDS IN CONTEXT**
>
> **conversion therapy**
> Therapy that seeks to change a person's sexual orientation from homosexual to heterosexual.

Scientific consensus is solidly against conversion therapy, declaring it not only useless but also harmful. All major American and international psychological and psychiatric organizations

Despite growing evidence to the contrary, many people still believe that sexual orientation can be changed using conversion therapies that may include psychotherapy, behavior modification, sex therapy, and more. Those who support such endeavors are often affiliated with fundamentalist religious groups like the one pictured here.

Hope

"Be strong and let your heart take courage,
All you who hope in the Lord."

have come out against the practice. The American Psychiatric Association, for example, states that it "opposes any psychiatric treatment, such as 'reparative' or conversion therapy, which is based upon the assumption that homosexuality per se is a mental disorder or . . . that the patient should change his/her sexual homosexual orientation."[45] The American Psychological Association, the American Medical Association, the American Academy of Pediatrics, and many other organizations have issued similar statements.

But this opposition does not deter supporters and providers of conversion therapy, who insist that their techniques work. Whether or not this is true, the argument can be made that people have the right to try to change their sexual orientation, if they so desire. "For some, religious identity is so important that it is more realistic to consider changing sexual orientation than abandoning one's religion of origin. . . . And if there are those who seek to resolve the conflict between sexual orientation and spirituality with conversion therapy, they must not be discouraged,"[46] declares one psychologist.

The Ex-gay Movement

This element of personal choice sheds a slightly different light on conversion therapy. For some people, circumstances or personal feelings make it prohibitively difficult to accept a homosexual identity and lifestyle. These people may enter conversion therapy out of desperation—and anecdotal evidence suggests that they often feel successful. About one-third of conversion therapy participants report that they have, indeed, become heterosexual as a result of their conversion efforts.

The ex-gay movement embraces people in this situation. Starting in 1973, various ex-gay ministries arose in America to support and encourage people who said they had made the shift from homosexual to heterosexual or who were actively working to do so. Some of these ministries are large national organizations; others are small and local. The support they offer typically takes a multifaceted approach, including discouraging people from entering or pursuing same-sex relations; eliminating homosexual desires; developing heterosexual desires; or entering heterosexual relationships. If all of these avenues fail, participants are encouraged to simply abstain from all sexual contact.

Opinions about the ex-gay movement are heated, both pro and con. Providers say their services are essential to their members' psychological and spiritual health—and many clients say they agree. Critics of the movement, on the other hand, say that ex-gay organizations promote self-hatred and damage the people they purport to help.

It is not possible to definitively state who is right and who is wrong on this issue. But it is indisputable that slowly and relentlessly, the tide of scientific and public opinion has been turning against the ex-gay movement and conversion practices in general—and at least some providers are listening. An ex-gay ministry called Exodus International, for example, had been in business since 1976 and, at its peak, operated about four hundred branches. However, in 2013 changing times and attitudes forced the organization to reevaluate its practices. This reevaluation led to the organization's closure and a shocking public apology from its president, Alan Chambers. "I am sorry for the pain and hurt many of you have experienced. I am sorry that some of you spent years working through the shame and guilt you felt when your attractions didn't change. I am sorry we promoted sexual orientation change efforts and reparative theories about sexual orientation that stigmatized parents,"[47] Chambers said at Exodus's thirty-eighth and final public meeting.

No Easy Answers

These comments were hailed by many as a huge step forward for the LGBTQ+ community, and it is true that Exodus's departure from the scene sent a powerful message. Ultimately, though, it did not answer the question of whether or not sexual orientation and identity could be changed. It was a concession to a growing body of evidence and opinion that, although substantial, does not enjoy a universal consensus.

Still, from the available evidence, certain facts do emerge. It is clear that sexual identity is more open to choice than orientation is; it is clear that both orientation and identity do change sometimes, often unexpectedly; and it is clear that deliberate attempts to change them fail much more often than they succeed, even if the participant is willing and eager. It will take time and further study to understand the roots of these findings. Whether biological, environmental, psychological, or a combination of all three, human sexual orientation and identity are complicated—and that, perhaps, is the only real answer.

SOURCE NOTES

Introduction: What Are Sexual Identity and Orientation?

1. Daniel Midgley, "How I First Realised I Was Straight," *Good Reason* (blog), March 9, 2012. http://goodreasonblog.com.
2. Anonymous, "Guys Who Say They Knew They Were Gay at Really Early Ages Are Lying, Right?," Data Lounge, Reply 33, November 17, 2010. www.datalounge.com/thread/9852379 -guys-who-say-they-knew-they-were-gay-at-really-early-ages -are-lying-right-.
3. American Psychological Association, "Answers to Your Questions: For a Better Understanding of Sexual Orientation and Homosexuality," 2008. www.apa.org.

Chapter I: Defining Sexual Identity

4. Brogan Driscoll, "I'm Attracted to Women as Well as Men, but That Doesn't Make Me Bisexual," *Huffington Post*, November 5, 2016. www.huffingtonpost.com.
5. *MainelyButch: Private Label* (blog), "Rules Don't Apply: Being Butch," December 13, 2016. https://mainelybutch.word press.com.
6. Lovely12704, "I Am a Femme Lesbian," Experience Project, June 24, 2013. www.experienceproject.com/stories/Am-A -Femme-Lesbian/3245576.
7. Kathy Belge and Marke Bierschke, *Queer: The Ultimate LBGT Guide for Teens*. San Francisco: Zest, 2011, pp. 13–14.
8. DollyDiva, "I Am Bisexual," Experience Project, March 20, 2010. www.experienceproject.com.
9. Quoted in James Dawson, *This Book Is Gay*. Naperville, IL: Sourcebooks, 2015, pp. 25–26.
10. Quoted in Lindsay Kimble, "Miley Cyrus on How She Discovered Her Pansexuality: 'My First Relationship Was with a Chick,'" *People*, October 11, 2016. www.people.com.

Chapter 2: What Determines Sexual Orientation?

11. A.R. Sanders et al., "Genome-Wide Scan Demonstrates Significant Linkage for Male Sexual Orientation," *Psychological Medicine*, vol. 45, no. 7, November 17, 2014.

12. Quoted in Michael Abrams, "The Real Story on Gay Genes," *Discover Online*, June 5, 2007. http://discovermagazine.com.

13. Simon LeVay, *Gay, Straight, and the Reason Why*. New York: Oxford University Press, 2017, p. 33.

14. Quoted in Patricia McBroom, "UC Berkeley Psychologist Finds Evidence That Male Hormones in the Womb Affect Sexual Orientation," UC Berkeley Campus News, March 29, 2000. www.berkeley.edu.

15. Quoted in McBroom, "UC Berkeley Psychologist Finds Evidence That Male Hormones in the Womb Affect Sexual Orientation."

16. LeVay, *Gay, Straight, and the Reason Why*, pp. 18–19.

Chapter 3: Forming a Sexual Identity

17. Mia, comment to Editorial Staff, "The Realization: How I Found Out I'm a Lesbian," The Other Team, 2017. www.theotherteam.com.

18. Quoted in Michelangelo Signorile, "Anderson Cooper Talks Coming Out as Gay, Brother's Suicide and GLAAD Awards with Madonna," OutQ, SiriusXM, March 11, 2013.

19. Fitjebirdy, comment to Editorial Staff, "The Realization."

20. Carrie Cutler, "When Did You Realize You Were Gay/Lesbian/Bi? How Did It Feel?," Quora, October 31, 2013. www.quora.com.

21. Jeff Pellarin, "What's It Like to Realize You Are Gay?," Quora, May 14, 2016. www.quora.com.

22. Gabriel Van Dekamp, "What's It Like to Realize You Are Gay?," Quora, May 23, 2014. www.quora.com.

23. Morgan Macke, "What's It Like to Realize You Are Gay?," Quora, July 31, 2015. www.quora.com.

24. Dan Holliday, "What's It Like to Realize You Are Gay?," Quora, July 10, 2016. www.quora.com.

25. Diana Cutaia, "'Coming Out' Starts Way Before You Say 'I Am Gay,'" *Wheelock Blog,* Wheelock College, June 25, 2013. http://blog.wheelock.edu.

26. Quoted in Patrick Strudwick, "'The Closet Is a Terrible Place' . . . How Coming Out Transformed Five Lives," *Guardian* (Manchester, UK), December 2, 2014. www.theguardian.com.

27. Quoted in Emily Blake, "I Am Cait: Is Caitlyn Jenner Attracted to Men?," *Entertainment Weekly Online*, August 6, 2015. http://ew.com.

Chapter 4: Life as an LGBTQ+ Person

28. C.G., "Why Is Being Gay So Hard?," Yahoo Answers, 2009. http://answers.yahoo.com.

29. Quoted in Eric Larson, "Internalized Homophobia: The Next LGBT Movement After Same-Sex Marriage," Mashable, June 25, 2014. http://mashable.com.

30. Quoted in Kelly Huegel, *GLBTQ: The Survival Guide for Gay, Lesbian, Bisexual, Transgender, and Questioning Teens*. Minneapolis: Free Spirit, 2011, p. 14.

31. GLSEN, *The 2015 National School Climate Survey Executive Summary*, 2016, p. 14. www.glsen.org.

32. Anonymous, "It's Not Easy Being Gay," *Express Tribune (Karachi, Pakistan) Blogs*, July 29, 2011. http://blogs.tribune.com .pk.

33. American Psychiatric Association, "Gender Dysphoria." www .psychiatry.org.

34. Quoted in Alyssa Jackson, "We're Not Caitlyn Jenner: Stories of Transgender Transitions," CNN, June 15, 2015. www.cnn .com.

35. Stephen Rainbow, "Why It's More Difficult Being Gay Today than It Was 20 Years Ago," EXpress: Your Gay Voice, 2016. www.gayexpress.co.nz.

36. JaviXO, "Coming Out Was Easy, Being 'Gay' Is Hard," Gaybros, Reddit, June 2016. www.reddit.com.

37. melizardbreath, comment to ANNarchy711, "Admitting to Myself That I'm Gay Is Scary," r/actuallesbians, Reddit, 2015. www.reddit.com.

38. Quoted in Ellen D.B. Riggle and Sharon S. Rostosky, *A Positive View of LGBTQ: Embracing Identity and Cultivating Well-Being*. Lanham, MD: Rowman & Littlefield, 2012, p. 128.
39. Quoted in Riggle and Rostosky, *A Positive View of LGBTQ*, p. 130.
40. Tyler Curry, "Six Reasons Why It Sucks to Be a Gay Man," *Advocate*, March 29, 2013. www.advocate.com.

Chapter 5: Can Sexual Identity and Orientation Be Changed?

41. Anonymous, comment to Debate.org, "Is Sexual Orientation Determined at Birth?," 2017. www.debate.org.
42. Freakoutimaninja235, comment to Debate.org, "Is Sexual Orientation Determined at Birth?"
43. Quoted in Rob Preece, "Former Prisoners Share Their Experiences of Sex in Prison," Howard League for Penal Reform, March 17, 2015. http://howardleague.org.
44. Quoted in Pepper Schwartz, "Can Sexual Preference Change with Age?," AARP, June 13, 2014. www.aarp.org.
45. American Psychiatric Association, "Therapies Focused on Attempts to Change Sexual Orientation (Reparative or Conversion Therapies): Position Statement," May 2000. www.psychiatry.org.
46. Douglas C. Haldeman, "Gay Rights, Patient Rights: The Implications of Sexual Orientation Conversion Therapy," *Professional Psychology: Research and Practice*, vol. 33, no. 3, 2002, pp. 262–63.
47. Quoted in Justin Snow, "'Ex-Gay' Ministry Apologizes to LGBT Community, Shuts Down," *MetroWeekly*, June 20, 2013. www.metroweekly.com.

FOR FURTHER RESEARCH

Books

Arin Andrews, *Some Assembly Required: The Not-So-Secret Life of a Transgender Teen*. New York: Simon & Schuster, 2015.

Ann Bausum, *Stonewall: Breaking Out in the Fight for Gay Rights*. New York: Viking, 2016.

Kathy Belge and Marke Bierschke, *Queer: The Ultimate LGBT Guide for Teens*. San Francisco: Zest, 2011.

Kirstin Cronn-Mills, *LGBTQ Athletes Claim the Field: Striving for Equality*. New York: Lerner, 2016.

James Dawson, *This Book Is Gay*. Naperville, IL: Sourcebooks, 2015.

Dan Savage and Terry Miller, eds., *It Gets Better: Coming Out, Overcoming Bullying, and Creating a Life Worth Living*. New York: Penguin, 2012.

Websites

Advocate (www.advocate.com). This site is the online arm of *Advocate* magazine, the premier publication serving and covering the American LGBTQ+ community.

Human Rights Campaign (www.hrc.org). The campaign is the largest LGBTQ+ civil rights advocacy group in America. Its website has a wealth of information on all aspects of LGBTQ+ life and issues.

It Gets Better Project (www.itgetsbetter.org). This project's mission is to communicate with LGBTQ+ teens and reassure them that things get better through inspirational first-person videos, many of which are available on this website.

The Trevor Project (www.thetrevorproject.org). The Trevor Project provides crisis and suicide intervention services for LGBTQ+ youth ages thirteen to twenty-four.

TrevorSpace (www.trevorspace.org). Run by The Trevor Project, this site is a safe social network for LGBTQ+ teens.

PICTURE CREDITS

Cover: iStockphoto.com/RapidEye

4: Maury Aaseng

7: Featureflash Photo Agency/Shutterstock.com

10: iStockphoto.com/kali9

12: iStockphoto.com/AmberLaneRoberts

18: Howard Lipin/ZUMA Press/Newscom

22: Shutterstock.com

25: Biophoto Associates/Science Source

29: monkeybusiness/Depositphotos.com

34: Stacey Newman/Shutterstock.com

39: monkeybusiness/Thinkstock Images

42: ginamcleanphoto/Shutterstock.com

49: Kurt_P/Depositphotos.com

51: nixki/Thinkstock Images

55: DMC/Splash News/Newscom

61: Lucy Nicholson/Reuters/Newscom

63: iStockphoto.com/lorenzoantonucci

67: Brian Cahn/ZUMA Press/Newscom

ABOUT THE AUTHOR

Kris Hirschmann has written more than four hundred books for children. She owns and runs a business that provides a variety of writing and editorial services. She lives just outside Orlando, Florida, with her husband, Michael, and her daughters, Nikki and Erika.